# FIND THAT BUG

# FIND THAT
# BUG

# Contents

# How To Find Bugs

This handy introduction to Australian insects will help you to find and identify the different families and species that you see, and enable you to tick them off as you go and keep a list.

All insects have six legs. It is useful to know one or two of the other body parts in order to help with identification – for example the 'feelers' on the head are called the **antennae**, the 'main body' section attached to the legs and wings is called the **thorax**, and the extended 'tail' section of the body is known as the **abdomen**.

Insect lifecycles are fascinating, with members of some orders such as butterflies and beetles producing caterpillar-like larvae, which then undergo **metamorphosis** in order to become winged adults. In other orders such as grasshoppers and true bugs the young nymphs are like smaller versions of the adults.

There are tens of thousands of insect species in Australia – there are thought to be more than 25,000 species of beetles alone! To help narrow down the identification possibilities focus on the shape and structure, the size and colour, and also the habitat and geographical location. For example, the Australian Painted Lady butterfly could be found almost anywhere in the country, in most habitats except for dense forest, but the Richmond Birdwing butterfly does not venture outside of a relatively small range mostly encompassing rainforest in south-east Queensland and north-east New South Wales.

The scientific names of the species, family or order are

often included in the text so that the bug can be researched further. If you want to find out more about insects it is well worth getting a comprehensive field guide such as *A Field Guide to Insects in Australia* by Paul Zborowski and Ross Storey or *A Field Guide to Butterflies of Australia* by Garry Sankowsky and Geoff Walker, which contain much more information and will help you to recognise every insect order and many families and species. Using binoculars for larger insects such as butterflies and dragonflies, or a magnifying glass for smaller less mobile insects, will enable you to get better views and make more accurate identifications. And a digital camera with a good zoom can help with identification later on.

# MAYFLIES

## ● Mayfly nymph

Order Ephemeroptera. Lives for several years underwater in streams, among rocks or in vegetation. Has three long tail filaments. About 10mm long.

## ● Mayfly adult

Order Ephemeroptera. Adults often hatch en masse to overwhelm predators. They live as adults only for a short time and have a dancing flight to attract a mate. Rests with wings held upright. Usually found near streams. About 15mm long.

# DRAGONFLIES AND DAMSELFLIES

## ○ Damselfly nymph

Order Odonata. Lives underwater in freshwater lakes, rivers and swamps. Narrow body, sometimes with three tail filaments. Predator of other underwater bugs. 12–18mm.

## ○ Dragonfly nymph

Order Odonata. Lives underwater in freshwater. Broader body than damselfly nymph and lacks tail filaments. Fearsome predator of other bugs and small fish. 15–25mm.

## ● Common Bluetail damselfly

*Ischnura heterosticta*. Long narrow body. Usually rests with wings folded back. Blue patch near tail-tip. Found Australia-wide near still or slow-flowing water. 30mm.

## ● Slender Ringtail damselfly

*Austrolestes analis*. Long narrow body. Often rests with wings folded back. Pale bands along greenish-bronze body. Occurs around lakes and slow rivers in south-west and south-east Australia. 31mm.

## ○ Orange Threadtail damselfly

*Nososticta solida*. Orange body and narrow slightly drooping abdomen. Freshwater habitats with some shade in eastern Australia. 35mm.

## ○ Whitewater Rockmaster damselfly

*Diphlebia lestoides*. Only in south-eastern Australia, from south-east Queensland to eastern Victoria, around faster-flowing streams and rivers in forested habitats. 40mm.

## Graphic Flutterer dragonfly

*Rhyothemis graphiptera.* Dark bluish body, red eyes and yellowish wings with bold dark markings. Rests with wings held open. Found around lakes, swamps and other wetlands across Australia. 40mm.

## Fiery Skimmer dragonfly

*Orthetrum villosovittatum.* Male has bright red body, female orange-red. Wings open when perched. Hunts small insects around wetlands. Found mainly in eastern and northern Australia. 35mm.

## ● Blue Skimmer dragonfly

*Orthetrum calenonicum*. Male sky blue with blackish tip to abdomen; female greenish-grey; outer wings of both sexes slightly amber. Occurs around wetlands Australia-wide. 45mm.

## ● Blue-spotted Hawker dragonfly

*Adversaeschna brevistyla.* Large, long-bodied dragonfly. Brownish with blue spots and blue eyes. Usually around bodies of still water but can wander far from wetlands. Australia-wide but absent from central areas and far north. 55mm.

# STONEFLIES

## ○ Stonefly

Order Plecoptera. Larva aquatic,
similar to dragonfly or mayfly
nymph. Adult sturdy with scaly
wings and long antennae. Nearly
200 Australian species, mostly in
and around fast-flowing streams
in uplands. 15–40mm.

# COCKROACHES

## ○ Bush Cockroach

*Ellipsidion australe*. Order Blattodea. Beautifully
patterned orange and brown. Feeds mostly on
plants: rarely seen on the ground. Found in
eastern Australia. 20mm.

# Desert Cockroach

*Polyzosteria* species. One of several species in the genus found in a variety of habitats across Australia.  These sturdy cockroaches are usually found clambering around in vegetation. 40mm.

# Trilobite Cockroach

*Polyzosteria limbata*. Also known as Botany Bay Cockroach. One of more than 500 Australian cockroach species, almost all of which are not household pests!
This beautiful-looking species is found in bushland areas in south-east Australia. 45mm.

## ● Giant Burrowing Cockroach

*Macropanesthia rhinoceros*. The world's largest cockroach, reaching 75mm. Shiny red-brown. Lives only in northern Queensland, where it plays an important role in recycling plant material in open forest habitats.

# TERMITES

## ● Termite workers

Epifamily Termitoidae. There are more than 300 species of termites in Australia. They live in colonies, with most species favouring sites inside timber, but a few producing spectacular earth structures. Workers are generally up to 5mm in length.

## ○ Winged termites

This is the reproductive stage of the termite life cycle. Once or twice each year the colony produces winged termites, which fly out on humid nights to form new colonies. 15mm.

## ○ Termite mound

Iconic earth mound produced by certain species of termites. One of the characteristic sights of the Australian bush. Can be up to 5 metres in height.

# MANTIDS

## ◯ Praying mantid

Order Mantodea. Note long adapted forelegs which are used for catching prey. One of more than 150 mantid species found across Australia in a variety of habitats. Adults usually 20–70mm.

## ◯ Garden Mantid nymph

*Orthodera ministralis*. Also known as Australian Green Mantid. Early-stage nymph shown here; strongly resembles ant. As it develops into adult it attains green colour and typical mantid shape with 'praying' forelegs. Nymph 7mm, adult 40mm.

## ● Giant Rainforest Mantid

*Hierodula majuscula.* Late-stage nymph shown here, adult female up to 100mm. Found only in rainforest and similar lush habitat in north Queensland.

# EARWIGS

## ● European Earwig

*Forficula auricularia.* Order Dermaptera. Pincer-like structure on tip of abdomen. This species widespread in habitats such as gardens and introduced from Europe; also nearly 100 native species. 20mm.

# CRICKETS AND GRASSHOPPERS

## ● Mole cricket

Family Gryllotalpidae. Sturdy forelegs for digging burrows. Very loud call at night. About 10 species around Australia. 30–40mm.

## ● King cricket

*Transaevum laudatum*. Family Stenopelmatidae. The only member of its genus. Found in the rainforests of north Queensland. 50mm. About 15 other species occur along the east coast. Related to the weta of New Zealand.

## Grass Pyrgomorph

*Atractomorpha similis*. Family Pyrgomorphidae. Also known as cone-heads for obvious reasons, there are about 25 species in Australia. Colours include green, brown or boldly patterned. 30mm.

## Blistered Pyrgomorph

*Monistria pustulifera*. Family Pyrgomorphidae. A widespread species of the Australian bush, favouring desert fuschias and occasionally garden species such as honeysuckle and privet. 40mm.

## Typical grasshopper

Family Acrididae. More than 700 species in Australia, with large variation in size and colour. Note long hindlegs for hopping long distances. Some species have wings, others lack them.

## Gum-leaf Grasshopper

*Goniaea australasiae*. Family Acrididae. Mottled orange-brown, resembling a fallen dead gum leaf. Often found in leaf litter, taking advantage of opportunity for camouflage. Eastern Australia. 30mm.

## ● Spur-throated Locust

*Austracris guttulosa*. Family Acrididae. Large nomadic grasshopper with patterned wings. Found Australia-wide and can cause damage to crops. 35–65mm.

## ● Migratory Locust

*Locusta migratoria.* Family Acrididae. Widespread species across Europe, Asia and Africa and also found Australia-wide. Suitable conditions can cause population explosions. 40–60mm.

## ○ Slant-faced grasshopper

Subfamily Acridinae. Lacks the structures on legs used for making typical 'chirruping' grasshopper sound, so also known as 'silent grasshoppers'. 35mm.

## ○ Gum-leaf Katydid

*Torbia viridissima*. Family Tettigonidae. Broad green wings resemble live gum leaf, even down to the central vein. Found in eucalyptus trees feeding on leaves. Nymphs resemble small brown ants. Adult 45mm.

## Bush cricket

Family Tettigonidae. About 1,000 species in this family in Australia, including bush crickets and katydids. Variable in colour but often green or brown. Found Australia-wide. 15mm.

# STICK INSECTS
# AND LEAF INSECTS

## Macleay's Spectre Stick Insect

*Extatosoma tiaratum*. Family Phasmatidae. Cryptic green or brown spiny body offers excellent camouflage in warm humid forests in Queensland and north-east New South Wales. Up to 140mm.

## Goliath Stick Insect

*Eurycnema goliath.*
Family Phasmatidae.
Huge stick insect.
Female larger than
male. Eucalyptus and
acacia woodland, and also
gardens, mostly in south-east Queenland and north-east
New South Wales. 100–200mm.

## Monteith's Leaf Insect

*Phyllium monteithi.*
Family Phyllidae.
Astonishing mimic
of leaves in the
rainforests of north-
east Queensland.
Very rarely
encountered in the
wild but has become
common in captivity.
55mm.

# CICADAS

## ○ Cicada nymph

Family Cicadidae. 250 species found throughout Australia. Spends six or seven years as a nymph underground drinking sap from roots, before the shorter-lived adult stage. As they hatch they leave an exuvia, or 'shell', which is often attached to a tree trunk. 25mm.

## ○ Red-eyed Cicada

*Psaltoda moerens.* Family Cicadidae. Nymph spends several years underground. Seems to emerge as adults in huge numbers some years, but be virtually absent in others. Mainly found in open woodland in south-east Australia. Sings continuously on hot days. 35mm.

## ● Green Grocer Cicada

*Cyclochila australasiae*. Family Cicadidae. Stout bodied and long winged. Calls from trees with a loud and piercing trilling which can be extremely loud when many call together. Eastern Australia. 40mm.

## ● Yellow Monday Cicada

*Cyclochila australasiae*. Family Cicadidae. A common yellow form of the Green Grocer Cicada. Calls loudly during hot weather or at dusk. 40mm.

# HOPPERS

## ⬤ Green treehopper

*Siphanta* sp. Family Flatidae. One of about 100 species of triangular-winged leaf-like hoppers. Found across Australia in habitats with lush foliage, from which the hoppers suck sap. 8mm.

## ⬤ Passion-vine Hopper

*Scolypopa australis.* Family Ricaniidae. Found on many species, including passion vines and lantana, where they suck sap. Winged adults look rather moth-like. 6mm.

# TRUE BUGS

## ● Assassin bug

Family Reduviidae. Predators of other invertebrates – here seen with pintail beetle prey. Has a distinct neck. 300 species found across Australia in many habitats. 12–30mm.

## ● Crusader bug

Family Coreidae. Oblong-shaped with raised margin around abdomen. More than 80 species in Australia. Later-stage instar shown here. 20–30mm.

## ● Shield bug nymph

Family Pentatomidae. Smaller versions of adults and not so shield shaped! Some species feed on plant sap, others are predators of other bugs. Sometimes forms crèches of young which are tended by adults. 5–8mm.

## ● Shield bug adult

Family Pentatomidae. Distinctive shield-shaped body. Also known as stink bugs because they produce a foul-smelling liquid in defence. About 400 species found across Australia. Generally 10–20mm.

## ● Seed bug

Family Lygaeidae. 400 species in Australia. Most feed on seeds or other plant matter, while a few are predators. Found Australia-wide. 10mm.

## ● Metallic Jewel Bug

*Scutiphora pedicellata*. Family Scutelleridae. Metallic green bug with red and black spots. Eastern coast of Australia, from Queensland to Tasmania. 10mm.

## Cotton Harlequin Bug nymph

*Tectocoris diophthalmus.* Family Scutelleridae. Also known as Hibiscus Harlequin Bug. Nymph is bright metallic green with orange spots. Sucks sap from plants, including commercial cotton crops, plus hibiscus, grevillea, bottlebrush and Illawarra flame tree. 9mm.

## Cotton Harlequin Bug adult

*Tectocoris diophthalmus.* The complete opposite to the nymph – a mostly orange bug with metallic green spots. Such is the contrast that adults and young were originally described as separate species. Found in eastern Australia. 16mm.

# WATER BUGS

## ● Pond skater

Family Gerridae.
Also known as water
striders. These insects
skate across the
surface of the water
using surface tension.
Preys on other insects
that fall into the water.
Can fly in order to find
new habitat. More
than 30 species found
all around Australia.
10–25mm.

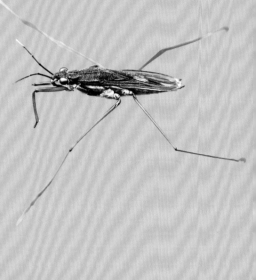

## ● Backswimmer

Family Notonectidae. Live underwater
and propel themselves along using
oar-like hindlegs for swimming.
Forelegs are used for catching insect
prey. 70 species of backswimmers
and the very similar water boatmen
(Family Corixidae) in Australia.
5–15mm.

# DOBSONFLIES

## ○ Dobsonfly

Order Megaloptera. Adults are large to very large with large broad wings. Often found near streams and larvae live underwater. Found all over Australia. 30–80mm.

# MANTISFLIES, ANTLIONS AND LACEWINGS

## ○ Mantisfly

Family Mantispidae. Smallish fly-like insects with the unique feature of long folded front legs that resemble those of a praying mantid. These legs are spiny and used to catch insect prey. 15–25mm.

## ● Antlion larva

Family Myrmeleontidae. Larvae live underground in sandy soils. They have huge jaws and are fierce predators of other insects such as ants. 5mm.

## ● Antlion larva pit

The female antlion lays eggs singly into sand. Once a larva hatches it buries itself in the sand and digs a perfectly conical nocturnal trap for prey such as ants, which fall in and are grabbed and eaten by the antlion larva.

## ○ Antlion adult

Family Myrmeleontidae. Adult looks a bit like a cross between a lacewing and a damselfly but with short club-like antennae. There are about 250 species in Australia, which can be seen on vegetation or on the ground. 28mm.

## ○ Orange Antlion

*Callistoleon erythrocephalus*. Distinctive with red head and forelegs and clear wings boldly spotted black. Note the club-shaped antennae which distinguish this as an antlion, as opposed to a lacewing. Found in eastern Australia. 25mm.

## ○ Blue-eyed Lacewing

*Nymphes myrmeleonides*. Family Chrysopidae. Long brown body, moderately long antennae and blue eyes. Larvae dig pits and catch insect prey in the same way as antlion larvae. 35mm.

## ○ Green lacewing

Family Chrysopidae. Green body, large transparent wings, long antennae and golden eyes. About 50 species found all around Australia. Often attracted to artificial lights at night. 20–65mm.

# BEETLES

## ◯ Ground beetle

Family Carabidae. Huge family containing more than 2,500 species which occur all across Australia in many habitats. Very variable in colour and pattern but generally have oval-shaped bodies. 10–90mm.

## ◯ Tree-trunk tiger beetle

*Distipsidera* species. Family Carabidae. Unusual for a ground beetle in that it is arboreal (found in trees). Active hunter of other insects in tropical rainforests in Queensland. 15mm.

## ● Rove beetle

Family Staphylinidae. Distinctive long narrow body. Also known as devil's coach horse beetles. At least 2,000 species in Australia – possibly double that number. 10–25mm.

## ● Golden Stag Beetle

*Lamprima aurata*. Family Lucanidae. Metallic golden-green. Named because male has extended antler-like jaws which are used for fighting. Found in dry forests in south-east Australia. 22mm.

## ○ Rhinoceros beetle

*Xylotrupes ulysses*. Named because of the spectacular 'horn'. One of 200 species of 'rhino beetle' in Australia. This species occurs in Queensland and is often found around poinciana flame trees. Adults feed on fruit. 55mm.

## ○ Three-horned Dung Beetle

*Onthophagus mniszechi*. Large dung beetle with rhino-like horn. Often found in and around sheep dung. Southern Australia. 15mm.

## Christmas beetle

*Anoplognathus rugosus.* Family Scarabaeidae. One of more than 30 species of Christmas beetles in the scarab beetle family. Named because they tend to be on the wing around Christmas time. 28mm.

## Fiddler beetle

*Eupeoecilia australiase.* Distinctive large black beetle with bold yellowish markings, named because the body is said to resemble a violin or fiddle. Often seen feeding on nectar on flowers. 20mm.

## Spotted Flower Chafer

*Neorrhina punctatum*. Looks superficially like a giant ladybird. Pale brown with bold black spots – patterning possibly aimed at mimicking bees – and feathered antennae. Eastern Australia. 24mm.

## Dusky Pasture Scarab

*Sericesthis nigrolineata*. Smallish uniform dark red-brown scarab beetle. Grasslands in southern and eastern Australia. Larvae feed on roots underground and can cause damage to pasture. 13mm.

## ● Ladybird larva

Family Coccinellidae. More than 500 species found across Australia. Larvae are slightly spiny-looking flightless bugs often found on leaves feeding on small insects such as aphids. About 5–10mm.

## ● Orange Ladybird

*Epilachna* species. Family Coccinellidae. Unusual among ladybirds in that the adults feed on leaves rather than insects and can sometimes cause damage to crops. 7mm.

## ● Fungus-eating Ladybird

*Illeis galbula*, Distinctively patterned black and yellow ladybird. Feeds on mildew, often found on the leaves of vegetable crops. Eastern Australia. 5mm.

## ● Variable Ladybird

*Coelophora inaequalis.* Adults and larvae feed on other insects. Sometimes used to help control crop pests such as aphids. Common and widespread Australian ladybird species. 6mm.

## Banksia Jewel Beetle

*Cyrioides imperialis*. Family Buprestidae contains nearly 1,500 species of often brightly coloured or metallic jewel beetles which occur across Australia. This species is quite large at about 35mm and is found in the east and south-east.

## Longicorn beetle

*Batocera frenchi*. Family Cerambycidae. A family of more than 1,400 longicorn or long-horn beetle species in Australia with long antennae that are often longer than the body. 10–75mm.

## ● Poinciana Longicorn Beetle

*Agrianome spinicollis.* Plain brown wing-cases and very long antennae. Common in Queensland and New South Wales. Found in rainforests and gardens, often around introduced Poinciana flame trees.

## ● Acacia Longicorn Beetle

*Penthea solida.* Medium-sized longicorn beetle with mottled black and white body and striped black and white legs. Larvae live in dead acacia wood.

## ● Weevil species

Family Curculionidae. Huge family of beetles with a distinctive elongated snout. About 8,000 species in Australia alone. Found in all kinds of habitats and ranging in size from 1–60mm.

## ● Botany Bay Weevil

*Chrysolopus spectabilis*. One of the most distinctive weevils, being blackish with powdery blue spots and stripes. Famously one of the first insects found and described after Cook's arrival in Australia. 25mm.

## ● Belid weevil

*Rhinotia semipunctata*. Long narrow-bodied species with
a pointed tip, identified as a weevil thanks to its distinctive
long snout. Found in eastern Australia. 15mm.

## ● Broad-nosed weevil

Family Curculionidae. Rainforest species from Queensland
with spines all over body for protection and camouflage.
18mm.

# FLIES

## ◯ Crane fly

Family Tipulidae.
Long bodies and
very long gangly
legs. Despite
resembling giant
mosquitoes they are
harmless to humans.
More than 700
species in Australia.
15–30mm.

## ◯ Tiger Crane Fly

*Nephrotoma australasiae*. One of the most distinctive
species of crane fly in Australia, with body boldly striped
yellow and black. 18mm.

## ○ Mosquito

Family Culicidae. Females feed on blood from other animals, including humans, to help develop the eggs. Notorious vector of diseases such as malaria and dengue fever around the world. 300 species in Australia. 7–12mm.

## ○ Moth fly

*Clogmia albipunctata*. Family Psychodidae. Small moth-like flies that inhabit damp places. Often found around sinks and showers, hence the alterative name of 'drain fly'. 3mm.

## Horse fly

Family Tabanidae. Family of over 200 species of medium to large flies, often with colourful compound eyes, which have a tendency to bite humans. Also known as March flies. 15–25mm.

## Robber fly

Family Asilidae. Distinctive long-bodied flies which hunt other insects in flight. More than 600 species in Australia. Variable in size, some quite large. 15–35mm in length.

## Small hoverfly

Family Syrphidae. Characteristic behaviour of hovering in the same position helps to identify these attractive little flies. There are more than 160 species in Australia, with many striped black and yellow, mimicking bees and wasps. 6mm.

## Bee fly

Family Bombyliidae. Over 400 species in Australia. Sturdily built hairy flies which often hover and rest with wings held in a 'V' shape. Often lays eggs on the larvae of other insects, which the bee fly larvae feed on. 12–24mm in length.

## ○ Bee-mimic hoverfly

Family Syrphidae. These large hoverflies are also known as drone flies. Their patterning mimics bees to deter predators, but they have no sting. All hoverfly species are important pollinators. 10mm.

## ○ Cactus fly

*Telostylinus angusticollis.* Family Neriidae. Very distinctive body shape and long legs. Typically found on the east coast of Australia near rotting vegetation, frequently in acacia woodlands.

## ⬤ Fruit fly

Family Drosophilidae. More than 100 species of these small flies. Larvae develop inside fruit. Often seen around fruit bowls, or around fruit in more natural environments. Many species have patterned wings. 3–7mm.

## ⬤ Bush fly

*Musca vetustissima*. Family Muscidae. Can be abundant and has an irritating habit of trying to land on people in search of moisture, especially around their faces and eyes! Larvae develop in animal dung. 8mm.

# CADDISFLIES

## Caddisfly larva

Order Trichoptera. Aquatic larva resembles that of a small dragonfly or damselfly but builds a protective case around itself using plant material or stones. Found in a variety of underwater habitats including rivers and lakes. 5–15mm.

## Caddisfly adult

Order Trichoptera. Rather moth-like with long antennae, but lack long curled proboscis (or 'tongue'). More than 800 species in Australia, usually found close to water. Generally 10–20mm in length.

# MOTHS

## ◯ Rain moth

*Abantiades argentata.* Blackish moth with bold white markings. Widespread in Australia but absent from many central and northern areas. Wingspan 40mm.

## ◯ Ghost moth

*Aenetus dulcis.* Green moth with orange hindwings. Female has two pale bands on wings. Found only in Western Australia, where the caterpillars burrow into stems of Swan River Peppermint. Wingspan 110mm.

## ● Processionary caterpillar

*Ochrogaster lunifer*. Also known as 'bag-shelter moths' after the habits of the caterpillars. Caterpillars have harmful hairs which cause severe irritation to skin and should not be touched. Small brown moth has white stripes.

## ● Wattle Goat Moth

*Endoxyla encalypti*. This huge mottled brown moth is superbly camouflaged against a tree trunk. Wingspan 150mm. Eastern Australia. Endangered. Caterpillars dig a hole in the earth and pupate underground.

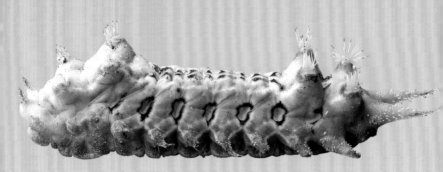

## ⬤ Painted Cup Moth caterpillar

*Doratifera oxleyi*. Spectacular multi-coloured spiny caterpillar that feeds on eucalyptus leaves in south-east Australia, including Tasmania. Small brown moth has dark borders to wings.

## ⬤ Southern Old Lady

*Dasypodia selenophora*. Barred brown moth with blue peacock-like eye-spots. Southern half of Australia. Caterpillars feed on acacia plants.
Wingspan 90mm.

## ○ Plume moth

Family Pterophoridae. Distinctively T-shaped moths with narrow feather-like wings. More than 40 species widely distributed across Australia in a variety of habitats. Wingspans 10–30mm.

## ○ Green Garden Looper caterpillar

*Chrysodeixis eriosoma*. Larva of small brown Geometrid moth, named after the looping action of the caterpillar as it moves along. Feeds on a wide variety of plants, including various vegetable crops.

## ⬤ Red-lined Looper moth

*Crypsiphona ocultaria.* Another moth in the Geometridae family which has looper caterpillars. The adult is cryptically patterned brown above but with bold red and black borders to the underwings. Common and widespread. Wingspan 30mm.

## ⬤ Wave-lined Geometrid moth

*Gastrina cristaria.* Moth brown with cryptic patterning. Larvae are bright green looper caterpillars. Widespread in southern and eastern Australia. Wingspan 45mm.

## ● Buff Bark Moth

*Gastrinodes bitaeniaria.*
Often found near eucalyptus
trees as these are foodplants
for the caterpillars. Mottled
pattern affords excellent
camouflage against bark.
Eastern Australia, from
Queensland to Tasmania.
Wingspan 40mm.

## ● Underwing Moth

*Achaea janata.* Underwings with eye-catching black and
white markings. Also known as Castor Semi-looper, after
the behaviour of the caterpillars as they move about. Wide
range of larval foodplants including castor, citrus, figs and
cabbages. Wingspan 60mm.

## ● Granny's Cloak Moth

*Speiredonia spectans.* Striking moth with distinctive large eye-spots. Eastern Australia from Queensland to Tasmania. Caterpillars feed on acacia plants. Wingspan 70mm.

## ● Four O'Clock Moth

*Dysphania numana.* Butterfly-like moth with yellow body and hindwing borders. Rest of wings blackish with blue markings. Often flies in late afternoon, hence the name. Wingspan 80mm.

## White-antenna Wasp Moth

*Amata nigriceps.* Body striped yellow and black. Wings black with transparent yellowish spots. Black antennae tipped white. Found in Queensland and New South Wales.

## Pasture Day Moth

*Apina callisto.* Orange body and brown wings boldly marked with white. Unlike the majority of moth species it is active by day rather than by night. Occurs in grassland in southern and eastern Australia. Wingspan 50mm.

## ○ Emperor Gum Moth caterpillar

*Opodiphthera eucalypti*. Often found around eucalyptus trees, as the spectacular spiny green caterpillars feed on the leaves. Found Australia-wide, although scarcer in south.

## ○ Emperor Gum Moth

*Opodiphthera eucalypti*. Adult pale brown with large eyespots on each wing. Female larger than male. Lives in adult form for only about two weeks before breeding and then dying. Wingspan 135mm.

## Hercules Moth

*Coscinocera hercules.*
Absolutely huge! Australia's
largest moth. Only found
in Queensland's tropical
rainforests, but also occurs in
New Guinea. At about 300cm$^2$,
the wings have the largest
surface area of any living insect. Wingspan 270mm.

## Convolvulus Hawk Moth

*Agrius convolvuli.* Wings mottled grey-
brown. Body boldly barred pink and black.
Crepuscular, meaning it is
often active at dusk and
dawn. Hovers at flowers
to drink nectar with long
proboscis. Migrants can
occur anywhere in
Australia. Wingspan
100mm.

## Vine Hawk Moth

*Hippotion celerio*. Striped brown and grey with a bold pale stripe down centre of each upperwing. Migrants occur Australia-wide. Wingspan 80mm.

## Vine Hawk Moth caterpillar

*Hippotion celerio*. Large green or brown caterpillar with eye-spots at head end, long blackish filament at tail end, and two pale whitish stripes running along top of body. Feeds on plants including grape vines.

# BUTTERFLIES

## ● Skipper butterfly

Family Hesperidae. More than 100 often very similar species found in grasslands, heaths and open woodlands across Australia. Wingspans generally 30–40mm. Species shown is Splendid Ochre, *Trapezites symmomus*, from eastern Australia.

## ● Darter / grass dart butterfly

Small skipper butterflies are found mostly in grassy habitats all around Australia. Colours usually orange and brown. Rather moth-like but identified by club-shaped antennae. Wingspans 20–23mm.

## ⃝ Richmond Birdwing

Family Papilionidae. Huge swallowtail, *Ornithoptera richmondia*, which lacks tail-streamers and is found only in south-east Queensland and north-east New South Wales. Wingspan up to 145mm.

## ⃝ Ulysses Swallowtail

Large swallowtail, *Papilio ulysses*, found only along the north-east coast of Queensland. Brownish underwings and long tail-streamers. Usually perches with wings closed but upperwings flash brilliant blue in flight. Wingspan 130mm.

## Blue Triangle

Medium-sized swallowtail, *Graphium sarpedon*, found in eastern Queensland and New South Wales. Lays eggs on laurel trees in forests and gardens. Often flies high in canopy. Wingspan 85mm.

## Chequered Swallowtail

Can migrate in huge numbers. A medium-sized swallowtail, *Papilio demoleus*, which lays eggs on citrus species. Often flies close to ground. Found Australia-wide. Wingspan 90mm.

## ⬤ Orchard Swallowtail female

Often found in citrus plantations. Male black with white bands near wing-tips, female more brown and grey. Large swallowtail, *Papilio aegeus*, found in eastern half of Australia. Wingspan 120mm.

## ⬤ Orchard Swallowtail caterpillar

Caterpillar spiny. In early stages camouflaged rather like a bird dropping and appears more black and white. Gradually acquires greener colour before pupating. Favours cultivated citrus plants and other species.

## Cabbage White

Family Pieridae. Introduced European species *Pieris rapae*, now occurs Australia-wide. All white with greyish wing-tips and one or two small black spots in centre of wings. Wingspan 50mm.

## Cabbage White caterpillar

Familiar with many vegetable gardeners as cabbages are among caterpillars' foodplants. Starts off plain green and as larva grows it develops brown ridges.

## ⬤ Cabbage White eggs

Small yellow eggs often laid in clumps on plants in the cabbage family. Found on cabbages in gardens and commercial crops such as canola.

## ⬤ Caper White

Native species *Belenois java*. White upperwings with broad black margins. Underwings blackish spotted with yellow and white. Lays eggs on caper plants. Wingspan 65mm. Australia-wide except south-west.

## Common Jezebel

Also known as Black Jezebel, *Delias nigrina*. Grey with black wingtips above, patterned with yellow and red below. Eastern Australia. Similar jezebel species found throughout Australia. Wingspan 70mm.

## Common Grass Yellow

*Eurema* hecabe. Lemon yellow with brown speckles on underwing and broad black tip on upperwing. Varied habitats from grassland to rainforest. Can form large groups on the ground. Northern half of Australia. Wingspan 42mm.

## ○ Lemon Migrant

*Catopsilia pomona.* Pale yellow with brown specks on underwing and dark edge at very tip of upperwing. Fast flight. Found Australia-wide except in far south. Caterpillars feed on *Cassia* plants. Wingspan 68mm.

## ○ Common Brown

*Heteronympha merope.* Family Nymphalidae. Orange with complex pattern of brown lines and small eye-spot on each wing. South-west Australia and from south-east South Australia to south-east Queensland, including Tasmania. Wingspan 72mm.

## Meadow Argus

*Junonia villida.* Upperwing brown with orange border studded with large eye-spots. Underwing plainer brown. Common in grasslands, woodlands and gardens across Australia. Wingspan 54mm.

## Leafwing

*Doleschallia bisaltide.* Underwing is a perfect imitation of a dead leaf. Upperwing orange with black tips – usually only visible in flight. Found along Queensland coast and in north-east New South Wales. Wingspan 78mm.

## Australian Admiral

*Vanessa itea.* Upperwing red-brown with black tips and yellow patches. Occurs wherever there are stinging nettles, which are the caterpillars' foodplant. Found Australia-wide except in far north. Wingspan 62mm.

## Australian Painted Lady

*Vanessa kershawi.* Common except in far north; sometimes migrates in huge numbers. Wings mottled orange and brown with black tips with white spots. Caterpillars feed on paper daisies. Wingspan 60mm.

## ● Common Eggfly

*Hypolimnas bolina*. Blackish with white egg-shaped spots.
Female also has smaller reddish spots. Forests and gardens
in eastern, northern and central Australia. Wingspan 95mm.

## ● Lesser Wanderer

*Danaus petilia*. Similar to Wanderer
but with less bold black veins
on wings and larger white
'windows' in black wing-
tips. Found throughout
Australia.
Wingspan 60mm.

## ○ Wanderer caterpillar

*Danaus plexippus.* Huge caterpillar boldly marked with black, white and yellow barring along the length of the body, and long black filaments at either end. Feeds on introduced milkweed plants from North America and Africa.

## ○ Wanderer

*Danaus plexippus.* A relatively recent arrival in Australia as the species expands its global range. Has fast low gliding flight. Can form dense colonies in winter. Found mostly in eastern Australia. Wingspan 108mm.

## ● Common Crow caterpillar

*Euploea corinna.* Feeds on a variety of host plants including oleander and a number of figs. Caterpillar is brown and finally barred with long black filaments. Found in northern and eastern Australia.

## ● Common Crow

*Euploea corinna.* Blackish with line of bold white dots forming a broken bar along the wing. Body spotted white. Can form huge roosts during dry season. Wingspan 83mm.

## ⦾ **Glasswing**

*Acraea andromacha.*
Named because of the
mainly transparent wings
which are boldly patterned
with black markings.
Seen in much of Australia
except for south-central
areas. Wingspan 60mm.

## ⦾ **Common Lineblue**

*Prosotas nora.* Family Lycaenidae.
Extremely similar to a number
of other species of lineblue
butterfly. Blue above and
finely barred brown and
white below. Caterpillars
are tended
by ants.
Occurs along
east coast of
Queensland
and New
South Wales.
Wingspan
28mm.

## ● Common Grass Blue

*Zizina otis*. One of many similar-looking grass blue species. Male blue above, female brownish. Underwing pale brown with darker brown spots. Caterpillars feed on pea plants. Found Australia-wide. Wingspan 28mm.

# WASPS

## ● Ichneumon wasp

Family Ichneumonidae. Large family of generally small, slender-bodied wasps, often with long antennae and a long egg-laying ovipositor, which resembles a very long stinger but does not sting! Various species occur Australia-wide.

## ○ Gall wasp galls

Superfamily Chalcidoidea. These tiny wasps lay eggs on a plant, which induce the formation of galls (as shown in the image), which act as protective 'nests' so that the larvae can develop inside. Many species occur across Australia.

## ○ Fig wasp

Superfamily Chalcidoidea. These tiny non-pollinating fig wasps are in the same family as gall wasps and the larvae develop inside figs. Many species across Australia, occurring wherever there are figs. 4mm.

## Braconid wasp

Family Braconidae. Huge and variable family, in which many species parasitise other insects, with the adult wasp killing them so that their larvae can feed on the body. For example, the *Calibracon* species shown here parasitises longicorn beetles.

## Cuckoo wasp

*Stilbum cyanurum*. Large metallic green cuckoo wasp – one of more than 70 species in the family Chrysididae. Parasitise other insects, with larvae feeding on other wasps or sometimes stick insects. This large species is 12mm.

## ◯ Spider wasp

Family Pompilidae. This 40mm-long individual from the genus *Cryptochelius* has paralysed a large huntsman spider and is carrying it back to the nest to feed its larvae. There are more than 200 species of spider wasps in Australia, ranging from about 15–40mm.

## ◯ Velvet Ant

Family Mutillidae. Parasitic wasps with wingless females which resemble ants in appearance and behaviour. There are at least 500 species in Australia, which parasitise social wasps and bees. 14mm.

## Flower wasp

Family Tiphiidae, which contains more than 700 Australian species. These are common garden wasps that lay their eggs in beetle larva. The winged male can sometimes be seen carrying the flightless female during mating. 20mm.

## Paper wasp

Family Eumeninae, containing 300 species of solitary wasps which build mud nests, often in gardens, and feed prey such as caterpillars to their larvae. 18mm.

## ◯ Potter wasp

Family Eumeninae. Boldly striped orange potter wasp female placing a caterpillar in mud nest chamber to feed her larvae upon hatching. 25mm.

## ◯ European Wasp

*Vespa germanica*. Characteristic yellow and black striped abdomen. Introduced species from Europe which is notorious for its aggressive behaviour and painful sting. Nests in large colonies. 22mm.

## ● Mud-dauber wasp

Very narrow 'waist' with bulbous tip to abdomen and curled antennae. Adults feed on nectar. Larvae live singly, each in a burrow, and are fed on other insects by the parents. This is a *Podalonia* species from South Australia. 22mm.

## ● Sand wasp

*Bembix* species from South Australia digging a burrow for a nest. Larvae live in colonies underground and adults feed them on insect prey. 15mm.

# ANTS

## ● Bull ant

Family Formicidae. Aggressive stinging ants
with famously painful stings! There are various
species from the endemic Australian genus *Myrmecia*.
Can grow very large for an ant – up to 20mm.

## ● Meat ant

Red Meat Ant (*Iridomyrmex purpureus*) attempting to drag
a dead fly to an underground nest hole to feed its young.
Endemic to Australia. Similar species found in drier areas
across the country. 10mm.

## ○ Sugar ant

*Camponotus* species. Mainly nocturnal and lives in large colonies. Likes to feed on sweet things, such as the secretions of aphids. Competitor with meat ant, and the two will attempt to kill each other and steal each others' food. 10mm.

## ○ Carpenter ant

*Camponotus* species. Foraging on dead wood on the rainforest floor, but can sometimes cause a problem for humans when it uses timber in houses as a substitute. 8mm.

## ○ Green-headed Ant

Australian endemic species
*Rhytidoponera metallica*,
which can be metallic green to
metallic purple. Widespread
across Australia in a variety
of habitats from deserts and
woodlands to gardens. 6mm.

## ○ Green Tree Ant

*Oecophylla smaragdina*. Brownish ant
with a green abdomen. Lives in trees
in tropical areas of Australia. Unusually
it constructs a nest from leaves joined
together with silk. 8mm.

# BEES

## ● Leafcutter bee

Cuts oval-shaped sections from leaves and takes them back to nest burrow. Various species in the genus *Megachile*, which are found all over Australia. Smallish bees at 8–15mm.

## ● European Honey Bee

Introduced bee, *Apis mellifera*, that nests in colonies. Abdomen striped brown and yellow. Domesticated to produce honey but some escaped to form wild populations. Today occurs across Australia. 15mm.

## Blue-banded bee

Solitary bees which nest alone rather than in colonies. Genus *Amegilla* with several species around Australia. Generally quite small at around 12mm.

## Teddy bear bee

Covered in dense orange-brown 'fur', including on legs. Striped abdomen. Scientific name *Amegilla bombiformis* – in same family as blue-banded bees.
Eastern Australia.
Often visits buddleia flowers. 14mm.

## Carpenter bee

Large wide-bodied black bee with furry black legs and bright yellow furry thorax. Eight *Xylocopa* species found in Australia. Loud buzzing noise draws attention to them. 20mm.

# SAWFLIES

## ● Sawfly larvae

Caterpillar-like grubs often in tight-knit groups, which can strip foliage. Some species, including this one, can irritate skin if handled, and are known as 'spitfires'. 10–70mm.

## ● Sawfly adult

Wasp-like. This species, the Bottlebrush Sawfly, has red and black stripes and is one of 200 sawfly species in Australia. Others are yellow and black, or brownish. Generally 15–20mm.

# Image Credits

All photos from Shutterstock.com – individual photographer names as follows (a = above, c = centre, b = below):

First published in 2022 by Reed New Holland Publishers
Sydney

Level 1, 178 Fox Valley Road, Wahroonga, NSW 2076, Australia

newhollandpublishers.com

A record of this book is held at the National Library of Australia.

ISBN 978 1 92158 053 6

Managing Director: Fiona Schultz
Publisher and Project Editor: Simon Papps
Designer: Andrew Davies
Production Director: Arlene Gippert

Printed in China

10 9 8 7 6 5 4 3 2 1

Also available from Reed New Holland:

*Find That Bird*  ISBN 978 1 92158 052 9
*Chris Humfrey's Awesome Australian Animals*  ISBN 978 1 92554 670 5
*Chris Humfrey's Coolest Creepy Crawlies*  ISBN 978 1 76079 445 3

For details of hundreds of other Natural History titles see
newhollandpublishers.com

Keep up with New Holland Publishers and ReedNewHolland:
 NewHollandPublishers
 @newhollandpublishers